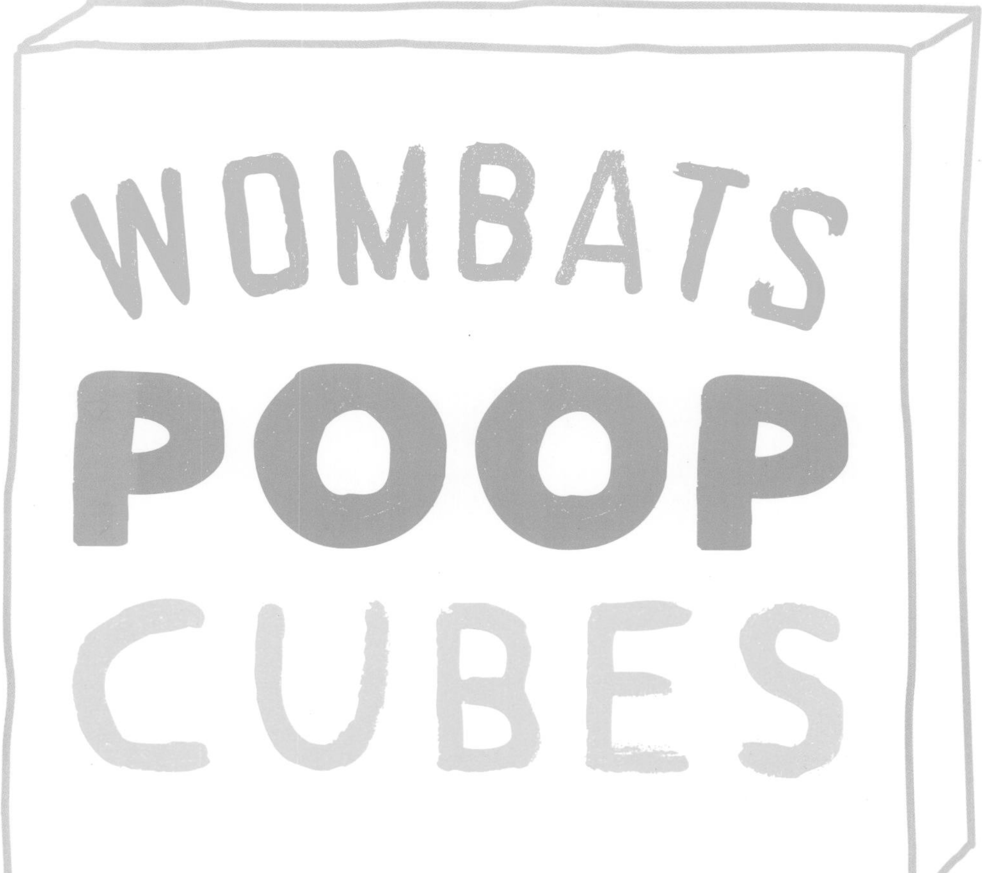
WOMBATS
POOP
CUBES

www.castlepointbooks.com

The Castle Point Books trademark is owned by Castle Point Publishing, LLC.
Castle Point books are published and distributed by St. Martin's Press.

ISBN 978-1-250-27071-9 (trade paperback)
ISBN 978-1-250-27072-6 (ebook)

Design by: Hillary Caudle

Images used under license by Shutterstock.com

Our books may be purchased in bulk for promotional, educational, or business
use. Please contact your local bookseller or the Macmillan Corporate and
Premium Sales Department at 1-800-221-7945, extension 5442, or by email at
MacmillanSpecialMarkets@macmillan.com.

First Edition: June 2020

10 9 8 7 6 5 4 3 2 1

WOMBATS
POOP
CUBES

SATURN RAINS DIAMONDS, PANDAS FAKE PREGNANCIES, AND OTHER MIND-BLOWING FACTS IN THREE WORDS OR LESS

KATIE ADAMS

CASTLE POINT BOOKS
NEW YORK

CONTENTS

FACTS:
FAST, NOW!

IT DOESN'T MATTER how long or how short it is, what truly makes a fact a fact is how, well, factual it is. Truth takes a lot of forms, and sometimes it only takes a few words to share an interesting bit of trivia or even tell a story. Fun fact: You only need three words to share a fun fact. Presenting *Wombats Poop Cubes*—which is a genuine, bona-fide full sentence—and also a book of totally trivial but fabulously fun and extremely interesting information.

But then again, there's that old saying from show business: Always leave 'em wanting more. When you read through this book of literally hundreds of three-word facts, you'll probably have more questions than the answers these short facts provided. Don't worry, you're covered— any and all facts have a story behind them, and these are no different.

So, please enjoy absorbing all these quick, shining gems of factualness about the world around you! Now read on and see just what the heck "wombats poop cubes" actually means!

CHAPTER 1

LIKE ANIMALS, THESE FACTS ARE
TINY AND INTERESTING.
(WELL, NOT THE LARGE ANIMALS.)

ALL CREATURES GREAT AND SHORT

RABBITS DISLIKE CARROTS.

RABBITS AREN'T ESPECIALLY FOND OF CARROTS, no more or less than any other vegetable. We only think they do because Bugs Bunny munches them all the time. And the reason he did it in the first place was a reference to the carrot-munching habit of Clark Gable's character from the 1934 movie *It Happened One Night*.

PANDAS FAKE PREGNANCIES.

PANDAS ARE AN ENDANGERED SPECIES and they're shy when it comes to mating. On the relatively rare occasion when a panda in captivity does get pregnant, well, it might just be fake. In 2015, Yuan Yuan, a giant panda at the Taipei Zoo in China, exhibited all the normal signs of panda pregnancy. Then an ultrasound revealed that the artificially inseminated Yuan Yuan wasn't really carrying a baby. So what's up? Experts say that pregnant pandas are so rare that they're lavished with attention and extras—particularly more, and better food—that Yuan Yuan falsified her pregnancy to get that special treatment.

ELEPHANTS SUCK TRUNKS.

LIKE HOW HUMAN BABIES, toddlers, and children will console themselves with the habit of sucking on their thumb, baby elephants do the same thing. They'll put the ends of their trunks in their own mouths to make themselves feel better when nervous.

MONKEYS FLOSS TEETH.

THEY *REALLY* HATE IT when they get a piece of banana between their teeth they can't get out with their tongue. So, they figured out a way to floss their teeth, long before humans invented thin, waxed dental floss. Monkeys use either blades of grass or bird feathers.

PLAYFUL
DOGS
SNEEZE.

HAVE YOU EVER been playing with a dog, and amidst all the bounding and running around the pooch has a sneezing fit? They aren't allergic to grass or dust or anything like that—they're trying to communicate with you. Dogs sneeze to let you (and other dogs) know that their biting and jumping isn't meant to be aggressive, it's out of play.

CHEETAHS DON'T ROAR.

CHEETAHS ARE CATS, and big, spotted cats at that. But while they have a lot in common with their domesticated cousins, one unexpected thing is that they make similar sounds. Unlike lions, cheetahs don't let loose with a loud roar, preferring to chirp, meow, and even purr.

SNAKES' TONGUES HEAR.

SLITHERY SNAKES don't have ears in the traditional sense. (After all, where would they go? There's nothing hanging off the sides of their heads, and no entry point, either.) This doesn't mean they can't hear. They do — snakes' tongues sense the vibrations caused by sounds.

PLATYPUSES SWEAT MILK.

AN INTERESTING CREATURE, the duck-billed platypus has feet like a duck, but is furry. They're mammals, and they nurse their young despite a complete and total lack of nipples. Female platypuses have mammary glands that secrete milk, which then oozes out across their skin, which their young can lap up at will.

DOLPHINS GET HIGH.

HUMANS AREN'T THE ONLY CREATURES on this planet that use substances to alter their realities. In other words, some people do drugs, and so do dolphins. They'll seek out pufferfish, which is toxic to them if consumed. But if they chew it, it delivers a disorienting head change (if you're a dolphin).

BATS AREN'T BLIND.

FORGET EVERYTHING you know about bats. Yes, they fly, but they are not birds. And sure, they look like rats, but they aren't rodents either. They're mammals. Also, the phrase "blind as a bat" is inaccurate, because bats aren't blind. They rely on echolocation to navigate, but their eyes work, although primarily in shades of gray.

FLEAS JUMP HIGH.

RELATIVE TO THEIR SIZE, fleas possess a superhuman (or super*flea*) level of jumping ability. Researchers at the University of Cambridge studied fleas' leaping ability, and they maxed out at seven vertical inches. That's more than 80 times the height of a single flea.

DOLPHINS NAME THEMSELVES.

RESEARCHERS HAVE NOTICED that dolphins will emit a unique whistling pattern. Other dolphins in their pod, or community, will then later repeat that pattern to communicate with and get that first dolphin's attention. In other words, dolphins have names that they use to refer to themselves and each other.

SQUIRRELS ARE ARBORISTS.

EVER WONDER HOW SQUIRRELS remember where they bury their acorns? Well, they usually don't. Scientists attribute the planting of thousands of new trees each year to squirrels who put acorns underground and forgot about them.

MOSQUITOS DON'T BITE.

MOSQUITOS DON'T ACTUALLY BITE YOU. They don't have teeth, but puncture the skin with a super-sharp proboscis. While they're collecting your delicious blood, they also urinate on you. (They've got to make room, it would seem.)

GLOWWORMS AREN'T WORMS.

BIOLOGICALLY, THEY'RE A TYPE OF FLY, more closely related to the gnat than anything else. Specifically, they're luminous flies. So while glowworms aren't worms, they do glow.

TURKEYS POOP SPIRALS.

WELL, NOT *ALL* TURKEY POOP IS S-SHAPED. Male turkey poop exits in a spiral fashion. Female turkey poop is shaped like the letter J. (So if you're ever wandering around a turkey farm, you'll be able to tell which is which when you avoid stepping on it.)

SLOTHS POOP WEEKLY.

SLOTHS' RELATIVELY RARE BOWEL MOVEMENTS are more a function of safety than necessity. The only reason these tree-hangers leave their trees is to roam down to the ground to poop. That's also the one time they leave themselves exposed to predators, so it's something they like to do as rarely as possible.

WOMBATS POOP CUBES.

IT'S A PRACTICE UNIQUE TO WOMBATS. These furry marsupials from Australia leave their waste behind to mark their territory — it's a kind of mating call to let other wombats in the area know that they're looking to breed. As it's a cube, it stays put to get that message out.

OTTERS
HAVE
POUCHES.

SEA OTTERS have a naturally-occurring pouch that grows in under their arms. It keeps out water and air and they use it for storage — usually as a safe place to keep pretty rocks they find. Really.

BASENJIS CAN'T BARK.

THE BASENJI IS A HUNTING DOG that originates in Africa. Because it has a narrower voice box than most other breeds of dog, the basenji is unable to bark. They do make plenty of noise, however. When excited in some way, they make a high-pitched noise comparable to a yodel.

BIRDS DON'T PEE.

BIRDS DON'T HAVE BLADDERS. A full bladder would be quite heavy, and could impede flight. Because they don't have bladders, they have no need for a urethra. Liquid waste leaves a bird the same way as its solid waste — all mixed up together, out the anus (and onto your windshield).

ECHIDNAS LACK STOMACHS.

ONLY VERTEBRATES — animals with backbones — have stomachs, and animals evolved to have them about 450 million years ago. The organ, and the acids it produced, broke down larger protein molecules. Over time, some animals lost their stomachs, including the spiny echidna and the platypus. Instead, their esophagus and intestine connect directly.

PENGUINS WERE MAN-SIZED.

IN THE PRESENT, penguins—those adorable, wing-flapping, black-and-white residents of Antarctica—stand about knee-high to the average adult human. They evolved to that size. About 40 million years ago, penguins were as much as six feet tall and weighed 250 pounds.

WHALES SLEEP UPWARD.

IT'S PRETTY HARD to swim and sleep at the same time, even for a creature that spends the entirety of its existence in the water. Sperm whales, for example, can only get comfortable by changing their horizontal position. When it's time to sleep, they flip to a vertical alignment and point their mouths toward the surface and just kind of bob around like that.

OYSTERS CHANGE GENDERS.

THERE ARE NO baby girl oysters — all begin life as males. However, by the time they're about a year old, oysters are females, because oysters can change their gender, not just early in life but at will for the remainder of their days. Because their reproductive organs generate both sperm and eggs, an oyster can fertilize itself.

ARMADILLOS ARE BULLETPROOF.

WE DON'T KNOW how anybody figured this out, but armadillo shells are incredibly strong. The shells have been known to deflect a .38 caliber bullet fired from a handgun, rather than have it go all the way through.

RATS
ARE
TICKLISH.

ACCORDING TO A STUDY at Humboldt University in Berlin, Germany, rats love to be tickled, particularly on the belly and on their feet. Those are also the most common places humans can be tickled, and also like humans, rats giggle when it happens.

CATERPILLARS ARE MUSCLEBOUND.

THOSE FUZZY LITTLE CRAWLERS are very agile, and so much of their body seems to move to make the tiniest of movements. Well, that's because the average caterpillar is packed with around 4,000 very small muscles. There are about 250 in the head alone, with around 70 in each body segment. A human only has about 630 throughout their entire body.

SNAKES CAN GLIDE.

THERE ARE FIVE SPECIES of snake collectively referred to as "flying snakes." The name is misleading because snakes don't really fly. (Whew!) Actually, they glide. Using a combination of free falling and twisting their body, they can grab ahold of a gust of wind and ride it to a new location. (Aaaah!)

TERMITES
ARE
FLATULENT.

TERMITES DON'T JUST FART A LOT, they fart more than any other organism on the planet. Fortunately, their flatulence is odorless. However, it does contain noxious methane, which is a greenhouse gas that's partially responsible for climate change. The tiny wood-chewers contribute as much as 30 percent of all the methane floating around in the atmosphere.

BEES GET DRUNK.

BEES POLLINATE a fragrant flower called the bucket orchid. One of the ways it entices bees to spread its pollen is by offering up a chemical that gets bees, well, intoxicated. Beehives are well aware of this phenomenon, too, because scientists have noticed that bee communities will punish bees that got drunk on bucket orchid chemicals or fermented nectar — other bees will gather round and rough up the drunk one.

JELLYFISH WILL EVAPORATE.

DEPENDING ON THE TYPE, jellyfish are anywhere between 95 and 98 percent water, and water evaporates under the hot, bright sun. If they wash up on shore and can't get back into the water, they can literally waste away into nothing.

PIGS RUN *FAST.*

PIGS HAVE THIS REPUTATION as slow and messy animals, but they're extremely spry, and among the quickest runners on the planet. They're sprinters more than they are long-distance runners. A domesticated pig can dash off at a speed of 10 miles an hour — way faster than even the quickest human athletes.

GENTOO
PENGUINS
PROPOSE.

YOU MAY HAVE HEARD before that penguins mate for life. That's not entirely true — some species pick one mate and stick with them for the entirety of a mating season. Some penguins, such as Gentoo, are more likely to reunite with their old partner year after year. Ninety percent of Gentoo thus "mate for life," and when they want to tell a penguin they've chosen them to couple up with, they'll present them with a pretty pebble.

PRAIRIE DOGS *KISS.*

THESE FURRY ONES have a unique way of greeting and identifying one another: they approach each other, lock mouths together, and kiss. Based on the kissing technique, the prairie dogs can tell if their kissing partner is or is not in their specific community. If they are, in fact, of the same ilk, they break up the kiss and walk away. If they're of different factions, they break up the kiss…and fight.

COWS HAVE FRIENDS.

COWS ARE APPARENTLY VERY SOCIAL, and when they feel stressed out or lonely, they'll take solace in their fellow bovines. Animal behavior scientists measured dairy cows' heart rates and cortisol levels and found that when they were separated from their herd, they indicated high levels of stress, which in turn led to decreased milk production.

REINDEER EYES MORPH.

IN THE WARMER, brighter summer months, reindeer eyes are golden. But in the colder, darker winter times, those eyes will change to a blue hue. The reason: There's a special layer in the reindeer's eye, behind the retina, that changes in response to the perpetual dim or darkness in the far north during the winter. That new blue eye allows more light in.

STARFISH
DON'T
BLEED.

ALSO CALLED SEA STARS, these five-pointed sea-and-beach dwellers don't bleed because they don't have blood. Instead, they have a circulatory system made up of what surrounds them most of the time: ocean water. It's pumped into the animal's vascular system through a sieve-like opening called a madreporite — it's that light-colored spot on a starfish's top side.

GIANT PANDAS BLEAT.

WHAT KIND OF SOUND do giant pandas make? They usually seem pretty quiet, and although they look like bears, they're not (they're more closely related to raccoons), so they don't growl. According to animal researchers, giant pandas will bleat — which sounds exactly like the call of a sheep. However, they only do this when they're ready to mate.

CAMELS PRODUCE MILK.

THIS IS EASY TO REMEMBER, because it rhymes: Camels are mammals. That means they can feed their young self-produced milk. Camels produce a lot of it, too. In one lactation session, African camels can give up to half a gallon of milk, while South Asian camels can make six gallons. One weird fact about camel milk: It doesn't curdle.

SQUIRRELS HAVEN'T EVOLVED.

NOW THIS IS JUST PLAIN NUTS. The squirrels running around our yards, gathering and hiding acorns and nuts, are nearly identical to the ones that lived nearly 35 million years ago. In other words, and unlike most every other animal on the planet, squirrels haven't kept evolving over the centuries — they were apparently just fine way back when.

VIRUSES CATCH VIRUSES.

VIRUSES plague all sorts of life on earth, with different ones affecting humans, animals, plants, insects, fungi, and bacteria. (Yes, germy bacteria can catch a germy virus.) In 2008, French researchers discovered a virus that was infected with *another virus*. A virus so large it can be seen with the naked eye called a *mamavirus* had been attacked with another, smaller, parasitic virus.

TERMITES
ARE
PICKY.

TERMITES EAT WOOD, but they don't like *every* kind of wood. For example, they love to chow down on spruce, pine, and Douglas fir. They avoid young cedar, but as it ages, the wood breaks down and termites are attracted to the resin-heavy decaying wood. They straight-up avoid bamboo, redwood, and ebony.

BATS GROOM THEMSELVES.

LIKE SMALLER, CREEPY CATS, bats are devoted to keeping their bodies tidy. Any time not spent eating, sleeping, or flying, bats will spend grooming. Biting and licking themselves keeps their fur clean, soft, and, most importantly, free of parasites. Some species even groom each other.

HONEYBEE QUEENS QUACK.

IT'S A PARTICULAR SOUND that sounds like what a duck does, although it can also sound like a sheep's bleat, a frog's croak, or a cat's meow. It's a behavior called *piping*, and it's a sound a virgin honeybee queen makes when there is more than one queen in the hive. It's a signal, or a callout, to the other queen to let her know that she's ready to fight to be the one-and-only queen.

KANGAROOS CAN'T REVERSE.

THESE POWERFUL JUMPERS from Australia are built to go forward, and with a lot of force and speed. They've got strong hind legs and muscular tails which propel them forward, and *only* forward. Those legs and that tail just don't bend the other way.

MACAQUES MAKE SNOWBALLS.

JAPAN IS HOME to these furry, cat-size primates that are similar to monkeys. They live in cold areas, and they more than earn their "snow monkeys" nickname. When it snows, young macaques will jump around in the powdery stuff, make snowballs and throw them at each other, and roll big piles of snow down hills.

ELEPHANTS GET HEARTBROKEN.

WHEN AN ELEPHANT DIES, their mate goes into deep mourning. They actually cry and collapse to the ground and refuse to get back up, even as other elephants in the pack comfort them and encourage them to stand up and move on. The heartbroken elephant just might stay down there on the ground, and refuse to eat...and eventually die, too.

CROWS
INVESTIGATE
DEATH.

WHEN A CROW DIES, other crows will investigate the scene of the crime, so as to see if there's some kind of threat to the rest of crow-kind. For example, if they see a human holding a dead crow, they'll "scold," which is a call of warning to the other crows as if to say, "beware this human."

TURTLE BUTTS BREATHE.

IT'S NOT JUST A BUNCH OF HOT AIR — some aquatic species of turtles can take in air through their anuses. Those turtles' butts are equipped with *cloacal bursae*, structures that are blood vessel-loaded tissues. The surface of these is so porous that it can absorb oxygen.

HIPPOS PEE BACKWARD.

THE HIPPOPOTAMUS is a *retromingent* animal, which means that they urinate backward. (Yes, there's a word that means "pees in reverse.") This means that their liquid waste sprays behind them, as opposed to hitting the ground directly underneath their bodies. Hippos do this to better mark their territory.

ALBATROSSES SLEEP MIDFLIGHT.

SCIENTISTS USED TO BELIEVE that albatrosses never stopped flying, for months on end, landing only to lay eggs and taking care of all other business while flying — including eating, mating, and sleeping. While there are records of albatrosses flying for 200 days at a time, they do land, albeit rarely. They do sleep while flying, but only in 10-second "power naps."

BARN
OWLS
SNORE.

THESE ANIMALS LIKE TO TAKE UP RESIDENCE where they can, in places like garages, and, well, barns. They're very sneaky about it, and people often don't know they have owl guests until they hear them snoring. It's a distinctive raspy, throaty noise — even baby barn owls do it — that can be heard from up to a few hundred feet away.

IGUANAS SNEEZE SALT.

MARINE IGUANAS LIVE ON BOTH LAND AND SEA, venturing out into the ocean to forage for algae. As they scarf down all that sea life, they wind up consuming a lot of salt, as well. Too much salt isn't good for those iguanas, so they have to get rid of it somehow. They have salt glands that collect excess sodium and violently propel it outward. In other words, they sneeze it out. (*Gesundheit.*)

FRIENDLY GORILLAS BURP.

GORILLAS ARE CAPABLE of more than a dozen different vocalizations, such as hooting, roaring, growling, screaming, and belching. When gorillas do that, they do it when approaching other gorillas. And they're basically saying, "Hello, I am friendly, and I mean you no harm."

PIRANHAS AREN'T PREDATORS.

SE MEAT-EATING FISH aren't monsters who will attack
evour humans if given half the chance. This is a myth that
s from Teddy Roosevelt. In 1913, he visited Brazil, where locals
essed their honored guest with a staged display of piranhas
ng on a side of beef. They'd actually stocked a river with the fish
hen starved them, ensuring they'd be ravenous when feeding
arrived. Roosevelt went back to the U.S. and wrote about his
unter with these supposedly dangerous and exotic fish.

SHARKS
CAN
BLINK.

THEY'RE THE ONLY FISH THAT CAN. However, they don't blink to moisturize or refresh their eyes; the massive amou of water that surrounds them at all times does a good job of tha Instead, their eyelids take the form of *nictitating membranes*. T covers the eyes when the shark most needs protection: while it' hunting, and while it's being attacked.

SHARKS ARE CANNIBALS.

SHARKS ARE BORN PREDATORS. Actually, they're predators even *before* they're born. A pregnant shark will carry a few shark embryos in her womb, during which time the most dominant shark emerges. That one will eat every other developing shark in there with it (all except for one). Why do they do this? Sharks can get pregnant by multiple fathers at the same time, and the sharks fight to be the one to continue on their bloodline.

CHAPTER 2

THESE FACTS ABOUT THE PAST
PROBABLY WEREN'T IN YOUR SCHOOL
HISTORY TEXTBOOKS...PROBABLY
BECAUSE THOSE THINGS WERE REALLY
LONG-WINDED.

A
BRIEF
HISTORY

ROOSEVELT
WAS
INKED.

THERE'S ONLY ONE PRESIDENT known to have had tattoos, and unsurprisingly it was the toughest one — the Commander-in-Chief who lead the charge up San Juan Hill, played football, went on hunting expeditions, and who once finished a speech after somebody shot him in the middle of it. He reportedly had the Roosevelt family crest tattooed across his chest.

NYC ALMOST SECEDED.

IN THE 1860s, as it is today, New York City was a hub of the American economy. And while the state of New York abolished slavery in 1827, the Big Apple-based textile industry benefited and profited from Southern-grown, slave-picked cotton. So as to preserve political ties to the Union and to not lose business with the South, New York City mayor Fernando Wood proposed in 1861 that the metropolis become a "free city," an independent nation who'd remain neutral in the Civil War.

GARFIELD WAS AMBIDEXTROUS.

PRESIDENT JAMES GARFIELD was only in charge of the United States for a few months in 1881 — he was assassinated — but he's still one of the smartest and most mentally agile individuals to ever hold the office. He was fluent in both Latin and Greek, and he could write one language with one hand *while* writing the other language with his other hand.

VIKINGS RAP-BATTLED.

THEY DIDN'T ALWAYS come at each other with swords or fists-a-flying. Rival Viking hordes also engaged in a practice called "flyting," in which they'd exchange insults...but they had to be delivered in the form of rhyming verse, and rapidly at that.

PEOPLE FEARED TOMATOES.

TOMATOES, a staple of several European culinary traditions, are not native to the continent. Explorer Hernán Cortés brought tomato seeds back from the Americas to Europe in 1519. In the 1700s, nobles and wealthy people ate those red, juicy fruits on those pretty plants...but then they stopped because it was common to die after eating them. They assumed tomatoes were poisonous, but really it was a reaction caused by the tomatoes and the lead in pewter plates. Consuming lead, not tomatoes, can be deadly.

HARVARD PREDATES CALCULUS.

CALCULUS, which enjoys a reputation as the toughest, highest level of math there can be, seems like the kind of thing they'd teach at Harvard University, one of the world's most prestigious and exacting educational institutions. But calculus wasn't part of the original curriculum — it couldn't have been. Harvard opened its doors in 1636, about 30 years before Isaac Newton and Gottfried Leibniz came up with this new math.

SHE
WASN'T
"POCAHONTAS."

THE NATIVE AMERICAN WOMAN famous for reaching out to the European settlers at the Jamestown colony in the 1600s, who married John Smith and returned with him to Europe, as made famous by the 1995 Disney movie *Pocahontas*? Yeah, that wasn't her real name. That was a nickname. Her given name: Matoaka.

NAPOLEON WASN'T SHORT.

SOLDIERS WHO FACED DOWN the French emperor's armies thought he was short because he surrounded himself with his Imperial Guard, made up entirely of extra-tall troops. When Napoleon died in 1821, his height was recorded as 5'2"...in French measurements. In English measurements, that translates to 5'7", making him about average for a French man in the 1800s.

LINCOLN POPULARIZED EMBALMING.

THE CORPSES of dearly departed Americans weren't usually embalmed until the late 1800s. After the tragic assassination of Abraham Lincoln, his body was sent by train from Washington, D.C. to Springfield, Illinois (his home state) for people along the way to pay their respects. In order to keep the body from, well, smelling, it had to be embalmed. As goes Lincoln, so goes America.

BUDDHA WASN'T FAT.

THE SPIRITUAL LEADER and central figure in Buddhism born Siddhartha Gautama was rather skinny. But over time, *Buddha* got confused and conflated with Budai, a 10th-century Chinese folk hero, and important in that region's form of Buddhism. All those chubby Buddha statues are a depiction of the heavyset Budai.

NINJAS WORE BLUE.

THOSE ANCIENT JAPANESE feudal warriors aimed to blend into the background wherever they went. Wearing a black outfit from head to toe (including a head-wrapping) would look pretty suspicious, so in the daytime, they wore whatever everyone else was wearing. But at night, to travel about undetected, they wore blue, not black. That's because the night sky isn't black, it's very dark blue.

COLUMBUS DISCOVERED HURRICANES.

OKAY, Christopher Columbus didn't come across the first hurricane known to man — just like how he didn't really discover America, because people already lived there and plenty of Europeans had been there before him to boot. But during one of his travels in 1495, Columbus and his crew encountered a weather phenomenon at sea that is obviously a hurricane. It's the first known description of one.

PIRATES CAPTURED CAESAR.

IN 75 B.C., about 30 years before he'd head up the entire Roman Empire, Julius Caesar took a boat trip to the Greek city of Rhodes to further his education. Pirates from Asia Minor intercepted the vessel, and kidnapped Caesar and put out a ransom. His friends back in Rome scraped the money together, and the pirates, true to their word, let Caesar go. Soon thereafter, Caesar put together a small mercenary army...and went after the pirates who'd kidnapped him. His crew killed the lot of them.

NOSTRADAMUS COULD COOK.

AS IT IS WRITTEN: In 1555, French astrologer and doctor Nostradamus published *Les Prophéties*, his famous (if not infamous) book of predictions of world events set to unfold over the next several hundred years. People are still trying to make heads or tails of his cryptic but spooky warnings, but the guy wasn't all doom and gloom. In the same year he wrote *Les Prophéties*, he also published a cookbook full of recipes for home remedies for medical maladies and cosmetics.

CARTER WATCHED PORN.

BACK BEFORE STREAMING SERVICES, one of the perks of being the president of the United States was the right to request virtually any movie and watch it right there in the White House. President Jimmy Carter watched a lot of movies during his 1977-1981 term, and in late 1977 he requested *Midnight Cowboy*, the 1969 movie about a male prostitute. It's the only X-rated movie to win Best Picture at the Academy Awards, and the only X-rated movie screened at the White House.

EDISON WAS HOMESCHOOLED.

CREDITED WITH INVENTING everything from the incandescent light bulb to the phonograph to the tattoo gun, Thomas Edison is one of America's greatest inventors and businessmen. It's especially remarkable in that he had very little formal education. After a school administrator told his mother young Edison was "addled" (a 19th-century word akin to an informal ADD diagnosis today), she taught him at home herself. She taught Edison everything he needed to know before he left home at age 16.

CAPONE PLAYED BANJO.

ONE OF THE FIRST INMATES in Alcatraz, the new island prison off the coast of San Francisco upon its opening in 1934: mob boss and tax-evader Al Capone. The austere, severe prison reportedly broke his spirit, and made him so docile as to behave. He was so well mannered that Capone, or rather convict no. 85, was allowed to play in the Rock Islanders, the Alcatraz prison band which gave weekly Sunday night concerts for the prison's other "guests."

CLEVELAND DRAFT-DODGED.

GROVER CLEVELAND served as president of the United States in two nonconsecutive terms, from 1885 to 1889, and again from 1893 to 1897. During the Civil War, he was a healthy young man of military service age, and was subsequently drafted to fight for the Union army. He never saw a day of combat, however. There was a clause in the Enrollment Act of 1863 that allowed men of means to pay $300 to have somebody else serve in their place, and so Cleveland did that.

EINSTEIN INSPIRED YODA.

THE TINY, wrinkled, green Jedi from the *Star Wars* movie was designed by special effects artist Stuart Freeborn. He modeled specific parts of Yoda's looks, particularly his eyes and wrinkles, off famous physicist Albert Einstein. Freeborn had a photo of the scientist hanging in his office, and imitated what he saw.

HEROIN WAS MEDICINE.

ONE OF THE MOST DANGEROUS and addictive drugs known to man, heroin is a derivative of opium. An English chemist developed it in 1874, and the Bayer Pharmaceutical Company put heroin products on drugstore shelves in 1898. Its chief purpose: To be a less addictive alternative to morphine.

BINGO WAS BEANO.

BASED ON A FRENCH GAME from the 1700s that in turn was based on an Italian lottery game from the 1500s, Bingo became a craze at parties and carnivals in the United States in the early 1900s. Except at the time it was called Beano, because of what players used to mark their cards when they matched a called-out number: beans.

OXFORD PREDATES AZTECS.

THE BRITISH ISLES have been inhabited and civilized for a very long time. They were once part of the Roman Empire, and the "modern era" of England unofficially begins with the Norman Conquest of 1066. Just 30 years later, the prestigious Oxford University began training the brightest and wealthiest students. Meanwhile, the massive civilization of the Aztecs really began in earnest with the founding of the metropolis of Tenochtitlan in 1325.

ABRAHAM LINCOLN WRESTLED.

BEFORE HE WAS A PRESIDENT, he was a lawyer, and before he was a lawyer, Lincoln earned his living as a wrestler. Records from the early 1800s are spotty, but the tall, lanky grappler reportedly won about 300 matches and lost just once. He even engaged in some WWE-levels of trash talk, once telling a crowd, "I'm the big buck of this lick. If any of you want to try it, come on and whet your horns.

ANCIENT EGYPTIANS BOWLED.

IN THE 1930s, an excavation of ancient Egyptian artifacts led by English anthropologist Sir Flinders Petrie uncovered the grave of an Egyptian child dating to about 3200 B.C. In that grave were some of the boy's personal effects, including a primitive bowling set, comprised of stone pins and a stone ball.

AGATHA CHRISTIE SURFED.

THE BRITISH MYSTERY author wrote more than 80 books, gave the world Miss Marple and Hercule Poirot mystery stories, and in 1924, while on a year-round expedition, learned to surf. Her diaries revealed that when she visited surf havens like Hawaii and Australia, she caught some tasty waves. "Oh, it was heaven! Nothing like it. Nothing like that rushing through the water at what seemed to you a speed of about two hundred miles an hour," she wrote.

LEONARDO ORGANIZED WEDDINGS.

LEONARDO DA VINCI was most famously an artist, scientist, inventor, and mathematician. He also worked as a wedding planner. Certainly his background in the food industry helped him prepare other people's wedding feasts between 1489 and 1493. One of his first events: the wedding of Duke Gian Galeazzo Sforza and Isabella of Aragon, which included the couple walking through huge representations of revolving planets that popped open to reveal a guest dressed as a Greek god or goddess.

NAPOLEON WROTE ROMANCE.

IN 1795, the French emperor Napoleon wrote *Clisson et Eugénie*, a romance novel about the ill-fated romance between a soldier and a woman. Napoleon probably wrote it about his own poorly ended affair with Swedish royal Eugénie Désirée Clary. The book wasn't translated into English until 2009.

MOZART HATED TRUMPETS.

AS A CHILD, Wolfgang Amadeus Mozart hated the sound and volume of trumpets. Seeing as how he was already composing music, this was a problem, so his father hired somebody to follow around young Mozart and play a trumpet when he wasn't suspecting it.

MATCHES
FOLLOWED
LIGHTERS.

WHILE THE LIGHTER seems like more advanced technology than humble strikable wooden matches, the lighter came first. In 1823, German chemist Johann Döbereiner created the first lighter using hydrogen and platinum. Three years later, English chemist John Walker devised the first friction-strike match.

RABBITS ATTACKED NAPOLEON.

IN JULY 1807, Napoleon wanted to celebrate the end of a war between France and Russia with a rabbit hunt. He asked his chief of staff, Alexandre Berthier, to arrange it, and he did, inviting military officers and gathering up hundreds of rabbits from farmers. The rabbits were released from their cages, and Napoleon and his men gave chase…except the rabbits didn't scurry away. Hundreds ran right at Napoleon. He tried to fight them off with sticks, but to no avail, escaping these bold bunnies only by riding away in a carriage.

NIXON
WAS
MUSICAL.

NO MATTER YOUR POLITICS, you have to admit that President Richard Nixon seemed more than a little uptight. It's a little surprising then that Nixon is probably the most musical American president in history. Nixon played five instruments: the violin, clarinet, saxophone, accordion, and, especially, the piano. He tickled the ivories in public on a few occasions, including playing "Happy Birthday" at the White House to celebrate Duke Ellington's birthday.

HAIRBALLS PREVENTED MURDER.

IN THE 1600s, European aristocrats and royals avoided attempts to assassinate them via poisoning by utilizing bezoars. That's another word for goat or sheep hairballs, and they'd put them in drinks, which would absorb any arsenic that might have been slipped in.

AUDUBON KILLED BIRDS.

THE AUDUBON SOCIETY is a famous charity that aims to preserve and conserve nature. It was founded by naturalist John Muir, who named it after John James Audubon, whose masterful, detailed paintings of birds helped educate generations about our fine feathered friends. To get the details right, Audubon had to observe his subjects. So how do you get a bird to hold still? Well, Audubon killed them, and then posed them.

WITCHES DIDN'T BURN.

IN THE UNFORTUNATELY REAL Salem Witch Trials of the late 1600s in colonial America, 20 people were found guilty of the crime of witchcraft, and were executed. Nineteen of them — all women — were hanged. Giles Corey, a man, was crushed to death by increasingly heavy stones. But nobody was ever lit aflame.

CHAPTER 3

JUST LIKE THE HUMAN BODY, FACTS
COME IN ALL SHAPES AND SIZES. (BUT
NOT THESE — THESE ARE ALL BRIEF
FACTS, BUT THEY ARE ALL ABOUT THE
HUMAN ANIMAL.)

LIFE IS SHORT

FETUSES GROW MUSTACHES.

WHILE THEY GROW IN THE WOMB, developing babies grow a thin layer of hair over their entire bodies called *lungo*. It starts as a mustache, and then goes all the way around. Just before birth, the baby sheds the lungo, then eats it. The baby's first post-birth poop is made up largely of this hair.

TATTOOS
AREN'T
VEGAN.

VEGANS DON'T EAT or use animal-based products in large part because they feel it's cruel to animals to do so — but sticking yourself with a sharp electric needle is cruel to you, a human animal. Nevertheless, the vast majority of tattoo inks aren't synthetically created. They're made from charred animal bones and animal fat.

BABY
BRAINS
TRIPLE.

FROM THE TIME OF A BABY'S BIRTH and up until their first birthday, their brain will grow to triple its original size. It continues to grow, although not as rapidly or profoundly, all the way up until about age 18.

BABIES
LACK
KNEECAPS.

IT'S TRUE, AND IT KIND OF MAKES SENSE when you think about it. Knees are vital to adults for walking, but babies don't walk until they're a year old or so, and before that they crawl. What will become kneecaps is actually just a bunch of loose cartilage in the middle of their chubby little legs. As babies learn to crawl and walk across toddlerhood, that cartilage hardens into knee bones.

EARLOBES ARE PURPOSELESS.

SPEAKING OF EARS, your side-of-head cartilage moves sound into the head where it can be processed by the inner ear and the brain. But what of earlobes? What purpose do they have? They're just flat little flaps of skin. That's actually *all* that they are — scientists haven't really determined why we have them.

FEARS AREN'T PHOBIAS.

A FEAR IS NOT THE SAME THING as a phobia. Fear is a natural, normal human reaction to anything perceived as a threat to one's physical or mental safety. A phobia is a psychological phenomenon, an overwhelming aversion to a particular, specific, even arbitrary object. Phobias are irrational, and people who have them even know that they're irrational.

SWEAT DOESN'T STAIN.

SAY YOU WEAR A WHITE T-SHIRT to the gym every day for a month and work out hard in it. At the end of that month, there are probably going to be some yellow stains on that shirt. That isn't caused by your sweat. Yellow pit stains are the result of a chemical reaction between the proteins present in sweat and aluminum, the active ingredient in commercial antiperspirants.

RAIN CONTAINS VITAMINS.

NOT ALL RAIN CONTAINS VITAMIN B12, but a lot of rain *can* contain vitamin B12. Rain isn't pure, unfiltered water — it falls through the air and runs off airplanes and rooftops, picking up microorganisms along the way. Those tiny creatures produce vitamin B12 as a byproduct of their metabolism, which comes out in the rain.

TASTE
BUDS
DIE.

YOUR TASTE BUDS WORK HARD, letting you know how everything you put in your mouth tastes, and they burn out quickly. They're in a constant state of death and rebirth, with the average taste bud lasting somewhere between 7 to 10 days before replacement.

CORPSES GET GOOSEBUMPS.

A FEW HOURS AFTER DEATH, the body begins decomposing, beginning with rigor mortis, a stiffening of the muscles and joints. As this happens, muscles contract, or flex, rather, making the hairs stand on end. That's the exact same thing that happens when a living person gets goosebumps, so in this regard, corpses get goosebumps.

VIAGRA STIFFENS FLOWERS.

ERECTILE DYSFUNCTION DRUGS work by widening vessels to allow for less restricted blood flow to, well, certain areas. The most famous ED drug, Viagra, or sildenafil, has a similar effect on plants. Research shows that if a "little blue pill" is dissolved in the water at the bottom of a vase full of blooms, the flowers will stand up straight and live an extra week, on average.

SKELETONS ARE WET.

THE PHRASE "dry as a bone" to describe something as being entirely devoid of wetness is entirely inaccurate, at least if the bone in question is a human bone. Bones are covered in a thin layer of tissue called periosteum, which delivers blood to the bones...and it's very moist.

INFANTS BARELY BLINK.

THE AVERAGE ADULT blinks 10 times a minute, or about every six seconds. Babies blink far less — only about twice per minute. Scientists aren't entirely sure why babies don't need to blink so much. As blinking helps eyes stay lubricated, one school of thought holds that baby eyes are naturally wet and don't need to be constantly moisturized.

YOUR INTESTINES RUMBLE.

YOU MAY SAY your "stomach is rumbling" when you're hungry, but that's not your tummy. The stomach is much higher in the chest, set behind the lower ribs. What's in your "belly" spot — and what rumbles during a hunger pang — is your small intestine.

BABIES *DON'T* DREAM.

BABIES' BRAINS ARE TOO IMMATURE to dream, plus they lack the life experiences that inform dreams. However, from birth, infants enter rapid eye movement or REM sleep, the deep sleep period that adults use to dream. For babies, REM sleep has a different purpose — the brain uses the opportunity to build and integrate pathways, particularly for understanding language.

EYES
AREN'T
BLUE.

BROWN EYES HAVE A BROWN IRIS, green eyes have a green iris, but blue eyes don't have any colored iris at all. The upper layer of the iris lacks pigment entirely, and it absorbs blue light in the invisible spectrum and traps it, thus presenting as blue.

GONORRHEA IS MIGHTY.

MOST FAMOUS AS A PERSISTENT sexually transmitted disease, gonorrhea is also, technically speaking, the strongest organism on the planet. A gonorrhea bacterium can pull up to 100,000 times its own body weight. That's the equivalent of an average adult human being able to drag a load of 22 million pounds.

GUILT DAMAGES IMMUNITY.

FEELINGS AND EMOTIONS can jump into the physical realm and affect the health of the rest of the body. A 2000 Study at Hull University in England found a correlation in people who felt guilty about small indulgences — eating too much dessert or sleeping in — with an increased susceptibility to contracting colds, coughs, and other viral illnesses.

NOSES
KEEP
GROWING.

AND NOT BECAUSE, LIKE PINOCCHIO, we're all liars. Most of the body's cells — bone, muscle, and fat cells, for example — stop duplicating in puberty, and so our bodies altogether stop growing. But not the nose (or the ears). The nose is made of soft tissue encased in cartilage, and that soft tissue never stops growing. So if you think somebody's nose has grown in their old age, you're probably right.

SWEARING RELEASES ENDORPHINS.

LETTING LOOSE with a litany of profane words following a surprise moment of pain — running into a table, or smashing your thumb with a hammer, for example — is a fairly common and understandable response. It's also natural. Studies show that swearing during a moment of panic and pain releases comforting chemicals called endorphins.

TREES AID HEALING.

IN A STUDY published in *Science* in 1984, researchers looked at patients recovering from surgery in a Philadelphia hospital over the course of a decade. They found that the ones whose windows looked out onto gardens, parks, or even a tree or two tended to heal faster.

YOU'RE
SLIGHTLY
BIOLUMINESCENT.

HUMANS GLOW IN THE DARK, and humans are also "day-glow." Albeit, it's in extremely small qualities, and the intensity of that faint light changes throughout the day. But you're likely never going to catch yourself emanating an eerie light in the middle of the night — our eyes would need to be about 1,000 times stronger to perceive that glow.

KISSING CAUSES WRINKLES.

THE SMALL WRINKLES that come in around the corners of the mouth and give off the appearance of a slightly frowning expression are called Marionette Lines, because they make a person look like that kind of puppet, which usually have hinged mouths. Marionette Lines develop over time as collagen in the skin breaks down and settles around the mouth. Time causes these, as do genetics, too much sun, smoking, and even overactivity of the mouth, particularly from kissing too much.

TUMORS GROW TEETH.

THERE'S A CERTAIN TYPE of tumor called *teratoma*, which is Greek for "monster tumors." Really. These things grow and contain all kinds of human tissue, including the kinds that grow into bones, muscles, hair, nerves, eyes, and the brain. They most commonly sprout teeth and hair.

TETRIS HELPS CRAVINGS.

APPARENTLY, you can curb one compulsive behavior with another one. A 2015 study by the University of Plymouth found that playing a game of the classic puzzle video game *Tetris* for just three minutes dampened test subjects' cravings for junk food and drugs by as much as 20 percent.

SUGAR CAN KILL.

THE OCCASIONAL SWEET TREAT is fine, but too much sugar all at once can overwhelm the body and shut it down. If you were to eat 500 teaspoons of the white stuff all at once, it would short out your pancreas and send you into a near-instantaneous and likely fatal diabetic coma.

BRAINS
ARE
FATTY.

THE BRAIN isn't made of memories and thoughts. All that grey matter and brain stem and such is about 60 percent fat. The rest of it: mostly water.

DANDELIONS ARE SCANDALOUS.

THE ENGLISH WORD FOR the pretty yellow flower is dandelion, but in French it's called *pissenlit*, which translates to "wet the bed." This is in reference to how dandelion leaves, such as when steeped and made into a tea, are a very effective diuretic.

ICEBERGS CONTAIN HEAT.

ICEBERGS ARE COLD, obviously — they're giant blocks of ice floating in extremely cold water. But there are so many molecules in an iceberg, and thus there are chemical reactions. Some of those generate a tiny amount of heat. Add it up together, and the average large iceberg contains about as much heat energy as would be generated by a match.

FETUSES HAVE FINGERPRINTS.

AS BABIES GROW in their mother's womb for nine months, it's their job to develop. Fingerprints appear relatively early, in just the 17th week of gestation. Those will be the fingerprints they'll have for their whole life.

CHAPTER 4

IT TOOK A LONG TRIP AROUND THE
GLOBE (AND BEYOND) TO BRING
YOU THESE TINY, TINY BITS OF
INFORMATION ABOUT THE EARTH
AND EVERYTHING ON IT.

IT'S A SMALL WORLD

DISNEYLAND FAKES FLAGS.

THE HAPPIEST PLACE ON EARTH proudly hoists the American flag in numerous places around the park. But look closely: They sport fewer than the standard 13 red and white stripes, and fewer than 50 white stars. That makes them not "official" U.S. flags. The reason Disney does this is to avoid legal flag-handling requirements. If they were actual flags, park employees would have to constantly raise and lower them, and hang them at half-mast during national mourning periods.

KENYANS LOVE COUNTRY.

THE MOST POPULAR RADIO FORMAT in the African nation of Kenya is country music, particularly old-school, classic country by the likes of Kenny Rogers and Dolly Parton. Musical anthropologists believe that there's a direct link between the African tradition of oral storytelling and country's tendency toward songs that tell a story. For example, Rogers' "The Gambler" and Parton's "Coat of Many Colors" are among the most requested and purchased songs in Kenyan history.

THE
MOON
SMELLS.

ASTRONAUT GENE CERNAN went to the moon on NASA's last mission there, 1972's *Apollo 17*. He brought back some samples of moon dust, and he claims that it smells like freshly discharged gunpowder.

IRAN
BANNED
MULLETS.

PEOPLE WHO LIVE IN the Islamic Republic of Iran cannot sport the "business in the front, party in the back" hairstyle made (in)famous by Billy Ray Cyrus and Joe Dirt. Along with ponytails and other "decadent Western hairstyles," the mullet was banned in 2010.

HOUSTON BANNED TUBE-MEN.

THOSE INFLATABLE TUBES with the arms that swing all over the place in the wind, usually found in front of car dealerships and strip mall openings, are banned in Texas's largest city. Sec. 28-37 of the Houston City Code was enacted in 2010, banning not just tube-men but other "attention-getting devices" including streamers and whirligigs.

WASHINGTONIANS RARELY MARRY.

THE DISTRICT OF COLUMBIA has a lower rate of marriage than every single one of the 50 states. Only 28 percent of men and 23 percent of women who live in the national capital are hitched, verses national averages of 52 percent and 48 percent.

ANTARCTICA WAS AUSTRALIA.

BEFORE EXPLORERS ACTUALLY LOCATED and explored Antarctica, it was merely a theorized landmass, referred to as Australia, an English version of Terra Australis, Latin for "southern land." In the early 19th century, authorities in New Holland decided they wanted a new name and went with Australia. The *old* Australia was then nameless from 1824 to 1890, when Antarctica was adopted.

RUSSIA DWARFS PLUTO.

THE (FORMER PLANET) PLUTO'S surface area is about 3 percent that of the Earth's...whose largest country by area is Russia. That nation, which spans both Europe and Asia, comprises slightly more land area than does Pluto.

TRITON WILL SPLIT.

NEPTUNE, the eighth and farthest planet from the sun, has 14 moons in its orbit. The largest of these is Triton, but it won't always be. Astronomers say that Triton is edging closer and closer to Neptune as it orbits and within 10 million years, that proximity will cause it to break apart and become a set of Saturnlike rings about the planet.

SAHARA: NOT SANDY.

WHEN YOU THINK "DESERT," you think vast seas of sun-soaked sand. That's only partially true of the Sahara Desert, the largest desert on Earth at more than 3.5 million square miles. It's got plenty of oases, mountains, and is primarily lined with gravel — only about 25 percent of it is sand.

GALAXIES EAT GALAXIES.

A GALAXY DOESN'T REST at a fixed point — it travels through space. As it does, it can and will collide with other galaxies. Galaxies pack tremendous gravitational pull, and two of them bumping up against each other will both try to absorb the other, but the one with the stronger galaxy will eventually win out, consuming and distorting the weaker galaxy. The astronomical term for this is "galactic cannibalism."

THE
SUN'S
WHITE.

IF IT LOOKS YELLOW, red, or orange, that's just a filtering effect caused by the earth's atmosphere. The sun is actually a gigantic ball of heat and energy that's all the colors at once, and when you combine all the colors together you get...white.

EVEREST IS GROWING.

MOUNT EVEREST isn't the tallest mountain on the planet's surface (the underwater Mauna Kea is bigger), but it's growing. It's about a foot taller today than it was 100 years ago — each year it puts on another 4 millimeters or so.

VATICAN CITY CLOSES.

THE HEADQUARTERS of the Roman Catholic Church is technically a sovereign, independent nation. It's also so small that it's essentially a district inside of the Italian city of Rome. At night, the Vatican locks its gates.

LOUISIANA IS SHRINKING.

LOUISIANA IS A COASTAL STATE, with some areas actually sitting at or below sea level. The state is also the natural home of the Mississippi River Delta, and levees control that river and protect inhabited and developed communities from flooding. Wetlands along the delta are built up by sediment delivered by the rushing river. The sediment washes out to the sea when the river flows into the Gulf of Mexico. About every hour and a half, an area the size of a football field washes out of coastal Louisiana and into the Gulf.

GOOGLE USES CAMELS.

THE INTERNET BEHEMOTH has an ambitious goal of mapping and photographing the entire world, so as to make its "Street View" as accurate as possible. It even captures the parts of the world that don't have roads. In the deserts of Africa, the company forgoes its camera-equipped cars and instead uses camera-equipped camels.

AUSTRALIA IS MOVING.

MANY LARGE LAND MASSES are slowly moving through the ocean and across the planet, but Australia is definitely the fastest. The Land Down Under may be the Land Up There in a few million years, because it moves about half a centimeter northward each month.

HAWAII IS EXPANDING.

HAWAII IS COVERED IN HUNDREDS of volcanoes, and many of them erupt continuously. The lava that flows out of those then merges with nearby ocean waters, chilling that lava into rock, and thus new land. Each year, Hawaii gains about 40 new acres because of this phenomenon.

SUBWAYS NAMED JAY-Z.

THE RAPPER, entrepreneur, and Beyoncé's husband was born with the name Shawn Carter. In picking his stage name, he found inspiration in his hometown of Brooklyn. There's a subway stop that's the intersection of the J and Z trains.

TESTAROSSA MEANS "REDHEAD."

THE FERRARI TESTAROSSA is among the fastest and most coveted sports cars in the world. The model name, or "redhead" in Italian, refers to how the heads of the car's engines are painted red.

HYUNDAI MEANS "MODERN."

THE COMPANY BEGAN as a construction firm in 1947 in South Korea. They soon found international success as a car manufacturer, a very modern idea considering the name of the whole thing translates in English to "modern."

NORWAY KNIGHTS PENGUINS.

IN 2008, THE SCANDINAVIAN NATION bestowed the honor upon a king penguin named Sir Nils Olav III. He resides at the Edinburgh Zoo in Scotland, where in 2016 he was again noticed for his service with a promotion to Brigadier by the Norwegian Royal Guard.

METALLICA PLAYED EVERYWHERE.

FORMED IN THE EARLY '80s, Metallica became one of the most popular rock bands on the planet, and subsequently entertained fans in the Americas, Europe, Asia, Africa, and Australia. In 2013, they played for a small group of about 100 research scientists at Carlini Station in Antarctica. Not only the first major band to perform on the icy landmass, that made them the first to play on all seven continents.

THUNDERSTORMS NEVER STOP.

IT'S A GREAT BIG PLANET, and there are a lot of weather systems floating around the skies. At any given moment, there are about 2,000 thunderstorms happening simultaneously, in different places around the globe. That adds up to about 16 million thunderstorms each year, altogether.

SATURN WOULD FLOAT.

BECAUSE SATURN IS MADE OF GAS and not much to speak of in the way of dense, solid material, it has an extremely low density. It's so low, in fact, that if you could put it into an absolutely gigantic swimming pool, Saturn would bob up and down in the water.

QUICKSAND ISN'T DEADLY.

DON'T LET THOSE OLD MOVIES and cartoons where people get lost in the jungle and drown in an unforeseen pile of quicksand fool you. Most all quicksand is only a few inches deep — not nearly enough to drown a person. (Also the "quick" is a misnomer — it pulls in its "victims" very slowly, so slowly that they can get out of it.)

SUDAN

CRUICIFIES

CONVICTS.

WHILE NAILING A PERSON ON A CROSS and exposing them to the elements while their body slowly and painfully expires is viewed as a particularly inhumane and ancient form of torture, crucifixion is still used in the African nation of Sudan as a form of capital punishment for murder and other serious crimes. It's also a legal although seldom used form of punishment in the United Arab Emirates.

COSTA RICA LACKS MILITARY.

AFTER A CIVIL WAR IN THE 1940s, the president of the Central American nation dissolved the military as a show of unity, with the money rerouted to social and cultural programs. The country has small forces of police around the country that enforce laws and border issues, but it has no standing armed forces.

TULIPS
ARE
TURKISH.

TULIPS ARE PROBABLY MOST ASSOCIATED with the Netherlands, likely because of the "Tulip Mania" speculation crisis that rocked the country in the 1500s. The lovely red and yellow flowers are actually native only to central Asia, particularly Turkey. They were first imported to the Netherlands, from Turkey, in the 1500s.

URANUS IS GREEN.

THE FARTHEST PLANET IN THE SOLAR SYSTEM (that you can't say the name of without giggling) has a number of interesting features. Firstly, it's green in color, caused by the abundance of methane in its atmosphere. That atmosphere is also the coldest of any planet's.

ICEBERGS ARE MULTICOLORED.

THEY'RE ACTUALLY BLUE, but only appear white because they're covered in snow. But they're not *always* blue. Particles of whatever is in the seawater that freezes into an iceberg can add a significant shade. Algae, rock dust, and other contaminants can make an iceberg green, black, blue, yellow, or even rainbow-striped.

ECLIPSES
CHANGE
WEATHER.

WHILE IT MAKES SENSE that a sudden partial or complete blocking out of the sun may cause the temperature to drop in the parts of the planet most affected by an eclipse, the astronomical phenomenon has an effect on wind and weather patterns, too. A 1999 eclipse in Europe lowered air temperature by as much as 5°F, causing a sudden change in the speed and direction of the wind.

TIES ARE CROATIAN.

IN THE 1630s, King Louis XIII of Paris met a group of mercenaries from Croatia (a future and now former part of Yugoslavia), and noticed that they all wore a long piece of fabric around their necks. He loved the look and introduced it to fashion-forward France, which adopted it into what's now called the necktie. The Croatian version is still around, and it's called a cravat, a word that's a combination of "Croatian" and *hrvati*, the Croatian word for Croatian.

BODIES COVER EVEREST.

CLIMBING MOUNT EVEREST, the tallest mountain on the surface of the Earth, is extremely difficult. While previous, extensive mountain climbing experience is certainly recommended, it's not required — the only necessity is paying about $50,000 in fees for the privilege. And so, not everybody who climbs Everest makes it to the top...or off the mountain. About 300 people have died in their attempts, and about 100 bodies remain on the mountain, and most of them almost entirely preserved by the icily cold conditions.

KARATE

IS

INDIAN.

THE ANCESTRAL HOMELAND and modern-day point of origin for the popular combat sport and inspiration for countless strip mall dojos is Okinawa, Japan. But it probably didn't actually start there. Some historians think karate developed in India more than a thousand years ago, and before it came to Japan it landed in China via an Indian Buddhist monk named Bodhidarma.

JEANS ARE *ITALIAN.*

INVENTED BY LEVI STRAUSS and Jacob Davis in the 1800s, jeans are named after the Italian city of Genoa, where a hearty textile called cotton corduroy, or *jeane*, was produced. More commonly, jeans are made out of denim, a material very similar to jeane. In the French city of Nimes, weavers couldn't re-create Genoese cotton corduroy, so they came up with cotton twill, or "de Nimes," which became "denim."

CHAPTER 5

SOME SMALL AND
DELICIOUS MORSELS
ABOUT FOOD.

JUST
A FEW
QUICK
BITES

EGGPLANTS CONTAIN NICOTINE.

NICOTINE IS A NATURALLY OCCURRING chemical compound found not only in tobacco, which is smoked to enjoy the substance's stimulative effects, but in other plants, too, notably the humble eggplant. But it's going to take a lot of eggplant to get a nicotine buzz going. Twenty pounds of the vegetable contains about as much nicotine as does one cigarette.

SKITTLES TASTE IDENTICAL.

"TASTE THE RAINBOW," as the multicolored fruit-flavored candy's advertising slogan implores? More like "smell the rainbow." A great deal of what we taste is smell. We also "eat with our eyes," and so the combination of odor and looks suggests to our brains that all the different fruit flavors in a bag of Skittles represent different flavors: orange, lemon, lime, strawberry, and grape. They're actually all flavored identically — they're just treated with different scents.

CHLORINE + SUGAR = SPLENDA.

THE TECHNICAL NAME for the sugar substitute is sucralose, and it was discovered by accident. In 1976, chemical company Tate & Lyle was testing industrial uses of chlorinated sugar — sugar molecules in which some atoms were replaced with chlorine. Non-native English-speaking chemist's assistant Shashikant Phadnis was asked to test one of these compounds, but misheard and thought his boss said "taste," so he did, and it was sweet (and it wasn't poisonous).

BANANAS CURVE SUNWARD.

MOST FRUITS ARE ROUND — oranges, apples, kiwis, and the like. Bananas are unique in that they're long, narrow, and thoroughly curved. How do they grow like that? Like a flower in a pot leaning toward a sunny spot to catch some solar nutrients, bananas curve as they grow, to face the sun.

YAMS
ARE
FLOWERS.

YAMS, often confused and used interchangeably with sweet potatoes, are a root vegetable that grows underground, much like the common "white" potato. And yet, yams are not sweet potatoes, and not even potatoes — they're a flower. They're a member of the lily family.

HONEY *TURNS* GREEN.

THINGS THAT GLOW under a blacklight are fluorescent. This means they absorb ultraviolet light, and then almost immediately re-emit that same light. A bit of that energy gets lost along the way, giving the light that does get emitted a longer wavelength than what got absorbed, making the otherwise invisible light visible and giving the material an eerie glow. One such material that does this: thick, porous honey. It makes sense that even light would get lost in that sticky mess.

RIPE
CRANBERRIES
BOUNCE.

EACH FRUIT AND VEGETABLE has its own unique way of letting you know it's ready for harvesting and eating. For cranberries, farmers take a crop of the fruit and drop them in a container with a piece of wood on one side. If they bounce up and past the wood barrier, they're ready to go. (What makes them bounce? Air pockets inside.)

SAMSUNG SOLD SEAFOOD.

TODAY IT MANUFACTURES and sells flat-screen TVs and smartphones around the world, but Samsung started out in 1938 as a small market. In the city of Daegu in Korea, Lee Byung-chul's company told primarily dried fish, locally produced noodles, and other groceries. It grew exponentially and diversified, only entering into electronics in the late 1960s when it began making black-and-white TVs.

FOOD AROUSES MEN.

ACCORDING TO A STUDY conducted by Chicago-based researcher Dr. Alan Hirsch, "food odors elicit the greatest sexual response" in males, more than any other scent-based stimuli. A combination of pumpkin pie and lavender increase penile blood flow by an average of 40 percent, while licorice and doughnuts together rated a 32 percent increase. Also ranking high: buttered popcorn, cheese pizza, and cinnamon rolls.

VINEGAR MELTS PEARLS.

THERE'S NO GOOD REASON to melt a pearl, as they're precious, valuable little gems that took a poor little oyster a long time to get right, but you can totally do it with some vinegar. A pearl is comprised primarily of calcium carbonate, while vinegar is acetic acid. That causes a chemical reaction, breaking the pearl down into calcium, carbon dioxide, and water.

GROWING RHUBARB POPS.

DUE TO A METHOD CALLED "FORCING," rhubarb grows in a field undisturbed for about two years. During this period, the plants convert solar energy to carbohydrates via photosynthesis and store it in their roots. During the second winter, farmers move rhubarb to a heated, darkened shed, "forcing" the rhubarb to use all of its stored energy to grow its stalks (the sweet, edible part). It does this so quickly that it makes a creaking or cracking sound.

FIGS AREN'T VEGAN.

VEGANS ARE NEXT-LEVEL VEGETARIANS. Not only do they not eat meat, they don't eat any sort of food product that has anything to do with an animal, even if the animal didn't die in the process of making it. That excludes things like eggs and honey, and, if they're going to be really strict, figs. But aren't figs just fruit that grows on a tree? Yes, but they often involve the death of an insect. The fruit is pollinated by wasps, who can get trapped inside the fruit...and absorbed into it as it ripens.

OREOS
ARE
VEGAN.

THERE'S NO CREAM in Oreo's famous "creamy filling." That's because it's not "cream" but "crème," and there are no dairy products or animal-based ingredients in the white stuff whatsoever. Nor are any eggs used in the cookie part — here's one junk food that's okay to eat, animal lovers.

BACON IS ADDICTIVE.

ACCORDING TO SOME SCIENTIFIC STUDIES, certain foods, particularly fatty foods like bacon (which consists almost entirely of fat, and a little bit of salt) are as addictive as hard drugs like cocaine. However, bacon is legal, won't give you an immediate heart attack, and tastes a lot better on a cheeseburger. Bacon and drugs are similar in that they overload the brain's pleasure centers, thus prompting a person to want to consume them more and more to re-trigger those pleasure centers.

POP-TARTS ARE *DANISH.*

HOW CAN THIS PERFECT EXAMPLE of breakfast fast food — a convenience food so simple that you don't even have to go to the trouble of putting it in a toaster to eat it — be based on a centuries-old homemade treat? Kellogg's got the idea for the wildly successful Pop-Tart from *hindbaersnitters*, a pastry that originates in Denmark. It consists of a thin pastry shell filled with fruit jelly and sometimes topped with just a bit of frosting.

CROISSANTS
ARE
AUSTRIAN.

THEY'RE ONE OF THE FOODS most associated with France's vibrant and historic food culture, but they were adopted by the French by one of its most famous citizens who was also not native to France. In the 1700s, Marie Antoinette of Austria became queen of France, and before the French Revolution and she was separated from her head, she introduced her new homeland to the croissant, a pastry invented in her homeland.

SPOILED EGGS FLOAT.

IF YOU'VE EVER GOT SOME EGGS in your refrigerator that became separated from the carton bearing their expiration date, there's a simple test you can do to tell how fresh they may or may not be. Place the egg in a glass of water. If the egg sinks to the bottom, it's fresh. If it floats, it's less than fresh. This is because eggshells are porous, and allow some air to get through. The older an egg is, the more air that's gotten inside of it, making it buoyant

SARDINES ARE HERRING.

THOSE INEXPENSIVE LITTLE CANS OF FISH are called sardines, but it has nothing to do with what kind of fish they are. There's no species of fish called sardines. What you're eating is actually herring. Sardines get their name because the herring canning process was developed on the Italian island of Sardinia.

COKE INVENTED COUPONS.

SHORTLY AFTER INVENTING and introducing his super-sweet, pep-restoring elixir in 1886, Atlanta businessman Asa Candler wanted to promote his newfangled Coca-Cola. So he handed out handwritten certificates good for one free eight-ounce glass of Coke at Atlanta soda fountains. (Value of that free Coke: 5 cents.) By 1913, Coke had entrenched itself in the national marketplace and was sold in every state, helped along by free Coke coupons. By that time, the company had given out more than 8.5 million coupons.

APPLES

ARE

ROSES.

THE ROSE, or Rosaceae, family is a biologically diverse and important one. Not only does it include the famous and ornamental rose flower, but it contains a number of edible fruiting plants, too. Apples are roses, as are pears, peaches, cherries, plums, strawberries, raspberries, quinces, and almonds. Yes, apples, roses, and almonds are all related.

ITALY IMPORTS PASTA.

MOST OF THE PASTA MAKING that happens in Italy — the ancestral home of pasta of all kinds — is of the small batch, handmade variety. Italy is a relatively small country, and can't match the manufacturing power of the United States. Most of the everyday, ready-to-go, boxed pasta that's on the shelves in Italy is the same stuff that's on the shelves in American grocery stores, and it's made in the U.S.A.

FOODS
AREN'T
BLUE.

BLUE OCCURS THROUGHOUT the natural world: in the sky, on the feathers of bluebirds, and in the water of the seas, for example. There are no known organic foodstuffs that are naturally blue in color. What about blueberries, you say? Those aren't actually blue — they're purple. (It's a wonder they don't call them purpleberries then.)

WASABI IS HORSERADISH.

TRUE WASABI, that super-hot sushi condiment, is made from the grated root of *Wasabi japonica*, a horseradishlike plant that grows in Japan, China, and Taiwan. The problem with real wasabi is that it only keeps its flavor and punch within 15 minutes after grating. Because of where it grows and its shelf life, it's impossible to ship it to the thousands of sushi restaurants around the world. That's why your favorite American sushi joint uses common horseradish, combined with mustard, starch, and green food coloring.

WILD RICE ISN'T.

THE GRAIN-BASED SIDE DISH isn't a type of rice, or even a kind of grain. Wild rice is technically *Zizania aquatica*, and biologically speaking it's a grass seed — because it varies in color, it looks like grains of rice that aren't uniform. It's also not wild. It's cultivated by farmers.

7-UP CONTAINED LITHIUM.

LIKE MANY OTHER SOFT DRINKS created in the late 19th century and early 20th century, 7-Up was marketed as a health drink. In 1929, Charles Grigg of the Howdy Corporation concocted a lemon-lime carbonated drink and named it Bib-Label Lithiated Lemon-Lime Soda. The "lithiated" part referred to how it contained lithium citrate, commonly known as lithium, a mood-stabilizing drug and early antidepressant. In 1936, the drink changed names to 7-Up, but kept the lithium in the mix until 1948.

NUTMEG IS HALLUCINOGENIC.

A LITTLE NUTMEG goes a long way. Only a pinch is necessary in even the most strongly autumnal pumpkin pie. It packs a wallop in other ways, too. If you were to consume three teaspoons of raw, unprocessed nutmeg (like picked off a tree and ground up on the spot and then swallowed), it can and will induce frightening hallucinations, paranoia, convulsions, severe nausea, and other unpleasant side effects. (Don't try this at home.)

PRINGLES AREN'T CHIPS.

THE UNIQUELY SHAPED CHIPS that come in a tennis ball can aren't technically or legally potato chips. They're marketed as "snack chips" because they don't fit the definition of potato chips. Real potato chips are made from thinly sliced potatoes, whereas Pringles are made from a dough comprised of potato starch which is molded into chip-like shapes.

NITROGEN CUSHIONS CHIPS.

THE AVERAGE BAG OF POTATO CHIPS seems to contain more air than it does potato chips. First of all, that air is nitrogen. It helps keep the chips from going stale, while also slowing the growth of bacteria. Nitrogen also works uniquely well as a cushion. That bag of nitrogen and chips is basically an air-tight pillow.

PEPPERONI

IS

AMERICAN.

WHILE PEPPERONI IS SIMILAR to other, authentically Italian cured dry sausages like *soppressata*, it's 100 percent American. It was developed in the United States in 1919, a combination of pork and beef and seasoned mainly with paprika, which gives it its distinctive red color. The word pepperoni is sort of Italian — it's the plural of *peperone*, Italian for "bell pepper."

EDAM

DOESN'T

SPOIL.

LIKE A LOT OF CHEESES, Edam is named after its place of origin — Edam, a city in the Netherlands. Pale yellow and coated in red wax, it was one of the most popular cheeses in Europe during the golden age of exploration (1300s to the 1700s) because it does not spoil. It doesn't go bad or get covered in mold. It starts off as a semi-hard cheese and just gets harder the longer it sits around.

POTATOES AREN'T IRISH.

THE POTATO IS A QUINTESSENTIAL ingredient in Irish cuisine and is strongly associated with the social history of the Emerald Isle — probably because the Irish potato blight of the 19th-century led to mass emigration to the United States. And yet, the potato is as naturally Irish as the pineapple. In 1589, famed British explorer Sir Walter Raleigh brought potato samples from the Americas and planted them at his estate near Cork, Ireland.

MANGOES CAN SUNBURN.

JUST BECAUSE THEY NEED THE SUN to grow doesn't mean that mangoes can't also get damaged by the sun. (They're kind of like people in that way.) Mangos left in particularly high temperatures with no shade can get "burned" by direct light. It manifests as a dry, shrunken portion along the skin.

HONEY DOESN'T SPOIL.

HONEY IS THE ONLY naturally occurring food — in that it's manufactured by bees — that's built to last. It's bees' food source during those long winter months. Not only does it have a very long shelf life, but honey contains almost no water and is full of sugar. That makes it a non-hospitable environment for the growth of bacteria.

POTATOES ABSORB WI-FI.

WHEN THE AIRPLANE MANUFACTURER Boeing started installing Wi-Fi on passenger jets, they couldn't very well test devices with a bunch of people sitting around for days on end, and instead used giant sacks of potatoes to locate Wi-Fi weak points on aircraft. It turns out that potatoes just as effectively conduct Wi-Fi signals as humans do.

GOLD

IS

DIGESTIBLE.

YOUR BODY CAN PROCESS GOLD, but it doesn't gain any nutrients or calories from it. The body's digestive system won't break it down. Instead, it will harmlessly pass through the intestines and be eliminated along with your other solid waste. While it's safe to eat a little bit of gold leaf used as a decoration on a dessert at a fancy restaurant, this doesn't mean it's safe to eat your wedding ring — gold jewelry is cut with other metals, many of which are toxic to humans.

CREAMER IS FLAMMABLE.

NON-DAIRY CREAMER, that shelf-stable powdered white milk substitute used to soften your terrible office break room coffee, is made up of a number of chemicals. One of them is sodium aluminosilicate, an anti-caking agent which keeps the powdered cream a powder. However, when that chemical goes airborne, it can become flammable. In other words, don't sneeze into a bottle of non-dairy creamer near an open flame.

CHEESECAKE IS ANCIENT.

THE DELECTABLE, super-rich dessert goes back to ancient Greece. A form of the dish very similar to the modern version was served as an energy-boosting snack to athletes competing in the first Olympics in 776 B.C. It was also a common treat at ancient Greek weddings. Ancient Rome adopted cheesecake from ancient Greece, and it stuck around and evolved through Europe over the centuries.

KETCHUP WAS MEDICINE.

IN THE 1700s, ketchup was a thick sauce made out of fish or mushrooms. In 1834, an Ohio doctor named John Cooke Bennet made a ketchup out of tomatoes. Because tomatoes are full of healthy vitamins, Bennet marketed it as a cure-all, claiming that it would eliminate diarrhea, jaundice, and indigestion. By the 1850s, it was obvious Bennet was exaggerating the health benefits of his product, and he went out of business. By 1900, this new ketchup joined its predecessors on the condiment shelf.

DIET COKE FLOATS.

OR RATHER, AN UNOPENED *CAN* of diet soda floats. That's especially interesting because a can of regular, full-calorie soda does not float. The difference between the two beverages is the reason for the discrepancy in floating ability: sugar. Regular soda packs about 40 grams of sugar, and it's a dense substance. It makes soda denser than that of water, causing the can to sink. Because diet soda doesn't contain sugar, its density is roughly that of water, and so it floats.

MACADAMIAS ARE AUSTRALIAN.

CLOSELY ASSOCIATED WITH HAWAII, where they're voluminously cultivated and harvested, macadamia nuts originated in the Land Down Under. They're native to Australia's eastern provinces and were first identified in the 1850s by German botanist Ferdinand von Mueller, who named them after Australian chemist and politician John Macadam.

TACO MEANS "PLUG."

IN SPANISH, the word literally means "plug," or "wad." How a folded tortilla filled with meat and vegetables came to be known as a plug, or taco, comes from the Mexican silver mining industry. Those workers used explosive bundles to blow away rock, consisting of a piece of paperlike material wrapped around gunpowder. Those were called wads, and when similar-looking culinary tacos developed, it only made sense to give them that name.

SALT
SWEETENS
GRAPEFRUIT.

HOW DOES THAT MAKE SENSE? Shouldn't *sugar* make grapefruit sweeter? It would, but it would also still taste bitter. Salt doesn't cover up or add flavor to a grapefruit, but balances out the ones naturally found in the fruit. Salt cuts the natural bitterness of grapefruit, thus bringing out its inherent sweetness.

CHAPTER 6

BIG THINGS COME IN SMALL PACKAGES.
AND SO DO REALLY WEIRD THINGS. IN
OTHER WORDS, HERE ARE SOME VERY
BRIEF BUT VERY ODD FACTS.

A LITTLE STRANGE

"RUBBER DUCKIE" CHARTED.

IN THE SUMMER OF 1970, the song "Rubber Duckie" from *Sesame Street* proved so popular that it was released as a single. In September, it peaked at #16 on the *Billboard* pop chart, credited to "Ernie" (but performed by Jim Henson).

PEZ
MEANS
"PEPPERMINT."

THE FIRST PEZ DISPENSERS were topped with rectangles, rather than cartoon characters and superheroes. The little candies weren't fruit-flavored either, they were peppermints — marketed toward smokers. "PEZ" is an abbreviation of "Pfefferminz," the German word for peppermint.

ICE
ISN'T
SLIPPERY.

WHEN ANY SORT OF PRESSURE is applied to ice, such as a footstep, it instantly melts the thin, top-most layer into water. That water is very cold, and that's what makes the surface of ice slippery, not the ice itself.

CONVERSE ARE SLIPPERS.

MOST SHOES produced by the company are coated in a thin layer of felt on the soles. The reason: This legally classifies the shoes as slippers. That saves Converse millions in tax dollars and tariffs levied on shoes...but *not* on slippers.

SPLASH POPULARIZED "MADISON."

THE 1983 MOVIE *SPLASH* established Tom Hanks as a movie star and Ron Howard as a director. It also influenced the culture with the introduction of one of the most popular names for American girls over the next 30 years. Daryl Hannah's mermaid character in the film is named Madison, and the name subsequently skyrocketed in popularity.

ALIENS CONTACTED ELVIS.

THE KING OF ROCK AND ROLL claimed that when he was eight years old, he was visited in his bedroom by aliens...who could see the future. They showed the young Presley what was to come in his life, which he said included images of himself as an adult performing on a stage in a white jumpsuit.

MULAN: DISNEY'S DEADLIEST.

BASED ON TALES FROM CHINESE HISTORY, the central character — and protagonist — of the 1998 Disney movie *Mulan* killed more people than any other Disney movie character. Throughout her various battles, Mulan killed an estimated 2,000 people.

ASTRONAUTS DRINK URINE.

THERE'S NOT A LOT OF ROOM on the International Space Station, and so resources are in short supply, too. Every inch of "space" must have a purpose, and since there isn't exactly plumbing in space, they have to figure out something to do with their urine. Result: Any liquid waste material left by astronauts, urine, in other words, goes through a purification and desalination process and is converted into potable, drinkable water for those same astronauts.

UNICORNS ARE BIBLICAL.

WHILE THEY'RE NOW FIRMLY a creature of fantasy, they merit nine mentions in the landmark English translation of the Bible, the King James version: in Numbers (twice), Deuteronomy, Job, Psalms (three times), and Isaiah. Did the authors of biblical books think unicorns were real? Probably not. The predecessor for unicorn in old Hebrew was "re'em," a word that refers to a specific kind of wild ox.

HAIL CAN KILL.

HAIL ARE ESSENTIALLY ROCKS made of ice that fall from the sky at a high velocity — the bigger they are, the more dangerous they are and more likely to cause damage to property and human beings. On April 30, 1888, a hailstorm ravaged the city of Moradabad in India. Hailstones were reportedly the size of apples and in some spots accumulated to two feet deep. More than 1,600 cattle and sheep died, along with 246 people.

FLAMETHROWERS ARE LEGAL.

THERE ARE NO FEDERAL LAWS in the United States that govern the ownership of flamethrowers, so as far as Uncle Sam is concerned, you can have one of these cool but dangerous Rambo-worthy weapons. On the state level, they're legal almost everywhere. Only California and Maryland have laws restricting ownership.

SNOW

IS

CLEAR.

SNOWFLAKES ARE MADE out of ice crystals, which are innately transparent. However, when light passes through these crystals, it tends to bounce and bend off of each and every individual crystal in that snowflake. That, in turn, reflects back the entire spectrum of light that's visible to the human eye, which our brains interpret as white.

MAGAZINES ARE RADIOACTIVE.

MOST PRINT PERIODICALS take on a glossy sheen that makes the pages shiny and smooth to the touch. That's achieved through a treatment of the paper with a kind of white clay called *kaolin*. It contains trace amounts of uranium and thorium, both of which are radioactive elements. (But don't worry — there's not enough in that issue of *People* to do any damage whatsoever.)

BATMAN WORE NIKES.

FOR THE 1989 MOVIE *BATMAN*, actor Michael Keaton's version of The Dark Knight wore what the character always wears: big black boots. But because producer Warner Bros. had signed a product placement deal with Nike, one of the biggest athletic shoe makers in the world, the studio had to incorporate sneakers into Batman's costume somehow. So, costumers fashioned Batman's boots from a foundation of black Nikes.

MYRRH

IS

SAP.

PART OF THE STORY of the first Christmas we've all heard forever is that the Three Wise Men brought three gifts to the newborn Jesus: gold, frankincense, and myrrh. The first two items are recognizable. But what's myrrh? It's a resin derived from a certain type of tree that grows in the Middle East. It's saplike and has a smoky smell, and was used for embalming and a variety of medical uses.

PEAT PRESERVES CORPSES.

WHILE MOST ASSOCIATED with Ireland, bogs full of peat, a type of moss, stretch across Europe, including Denmark, Germany, England, and the Netherlands. Another surprising fact about these peat bogs is that they can keep a dead body fresh and clean seemingly forever. In 1950, peat cutters in Denmark discovered a body in a bog, and the relative "freshness" of the body led them to believe it was a recent murder victim. An investigation revealed it was more than 2,000 years old.

CPR

IS

INEFFECTIVE.

YOU'VE PROBABLY SEEN CPR revive someone in countless movies and on TV. Sadly, this isn't an accurate portrayal of cardiopulmonary resuscitation. According to a 2014 poll, most respondents estimated the post-CPR survival rate at 75 percent. But no — a person who receives CPR gets their heart going just long enough to get them to a hospital. After that, things can and usually do go wrong. Only 10.6 percent of CPR recipients walk out of that hospital.

HELIUM DOESN'T FREEZE.

AT A TEMPERATURE OF ABSOLUTE ZERO on the Kelvin scale (that's -459.67° F), most every element on the periodic table in a liquid state will turn to a solid state...or freeze, in other words. But not the first element, helium. However, it will turn from a liquid into a solid when high pressure is applied (but not from low temperatures).

DYNAMITE CONTAINS PEANUTS.

IT DOESN'T NECESSARILY, but dynamite can be made in part via a peanut byproduct. If you want to make dynamite at home with peanuts, you'd first have to convert those peanuts into peanut oil. Peanut oil can then be made into glycerol, a vital ingredient in nitroglycerine, the explosive material that makes dynamite go *kaboom*.

CLOUDS WEIGH MILLIONS.

THEY ONLY LOOK LIGHT AND FLUFFY. Clouds are actually huge. Your average puffy cumulus cloud takes up about a square kilometer of space in the sky. Inside, there's a volume of a billion cubic meters, and most of that is water. That adds up to an average cloud weight of well over a million pounds.

A LITTLE STRANGE

MIRAGES
ARE
PHOTOGRAPHABLE.

MIRAGES AREN'T TRICKS of the imagination, or the mind playing tricks on you — they're the result of hot air swirling near the ground, resulting in some weird visuals. And if your eye can see those weird tricks of air and light that sometimes look like pools of water, then the mechanism in a camera lens will see it that way, too — so go ahead and take a photo.

THERE'S BRAILLE PLAYBOY.

THERE'S AN OLD CLICHÉ guys say when caught with an issue of *Playboy* in their possession: "I only read it for the articles." Sure, the magazine's most famous content is its pictorials of naked women, but it really does have a fine journalistic tradition, publishing highbrow fiction, investigative news stories, and in-depth interviews with leaders in politics, thought, and culture. As such, *Playboy* started publishing a Braille version in 1970. The publishers never translated the pictures into those readable bumps for blind readers, just the articles.

NASA BANNED BEANS.

AS NASA WORKED TOWARD sending astronauts to the moon in the 1960s, it consulted flatulence researcher Edwin Murphy. He recommended NASA hire only individuals who rarely farted. The reason: Farts contain methane, which is flammable, which could cause a major safety issue on spacecraft. Instead, NASA found the best candidates for their *Apollo* missions and simply banned astronauts from eating flatulence-causing foods like cabbage, broccoli, and beans.

TREES
BREAK
WIND.

MICROBES IN THE HUMAN BODY break down food and create gas, which is released as flatulence. The same things happen in the inner workings of trees. That methane slowly (and quietly) finds its way out through the stems or bark of a tree.

HEATED MAGNETS DEMAGNETIZE.

HOW DO YOU TURN A MAGNET into just a useless piece of material? Apply heat. If a magnet is heated to a temperature above 176° F, it will lose its ability to attract metal and make it stick. That demagnetization becomes permanent the longer the heat is applied, or the higher the temperature gets.

KARAOKE
IS
UNPATENTED.

JAPANESE MUSICIAN DAISUKE INOUE invented the first karaoke machine in 1971. Within a year, it was a smash hit, with 25,000 of them installed in Japanese businesses and homes within just a few years...not to mention similar machines made by companies other than Inoue's. He never bothered to get a patent on his machine, a worldwide sensation that allowed regular people to sing along to prerecorded music, forgoing likely hundreds of millions in royalties.

ARMAGEDDON TRAINS ENGINEERS.

THE 1998 MOVIE *ARMAGEDDON* is a fun blockbuster that totally sells its absurd premise: A huge asteroid is headed for Earth, so NASA sends a bunch of guys up in space to land on it and blow it up. Unsurprisingly, *Armageddon* is not exactly scientifically accurate in its storytelling, so much so that the real-life NASA uses it as a kind of anti-training film. Experts at the space agency count 168 scientifically impossible things in the film, and when they hire new engineers, they try to see how many they can spot.

ASTRONAUTS CELEBRATE CHRISTMAS.

ASTRONAUTS ASSIGNED TO THE International Space Station are there for months at a time, and the winter holidays may take place during that period. But they "deck the halls," so to speak, astronaut style. Scheduled payload deliveries include Christmas presents from loved ones back on earth, and the astronauts don't have to do any work on the big day, and instead hang out and eat a nice meal.

A LITTLE STRANGE

LISTERINE MADE CIGARETTES.

LISTERINE CLAIMS TO KILL nasty mouth germs with its harsh mouthwash products, but back in the 1930s, there was another semi-medicinal product bearing the Listerine brand name: Listerine Cigarettes. They were made from tobacco infused with "antiseptic essential oils" that promised to be "pleasantly cooling and soothing to the throat."

TOOTHPASTE CONTAINS ANTIFREEZE.

TOOTHPASTE HAS TO LAST inside that tube, and manufacturers include a humectant, a chemical that prevents the stuff from drying out. A commonly used humectant: propylene glycol. This is also the active ingredient in industrial antifreeze products, and when mixed with water, it's the stuff you buy to pour into your car each winter.

HULK

CHANGE

NAME!

"HULK SMASH!" the monosyllabic Incredible Hulk says before he, well, smashes. But Hulk do lots of other things, like get new name! Producers of the 1970s *The Incredible Hulk* TV series thought the Hulk's mild-mannered scientist alter ego Bruce Banner had a name that too strongly reeked of comic books. Indeed, alliterative names are common in comic books — Peter Parker, Lois Lane, and Lex Luthor, for example. So, for the TV version, Bruce Banner became *David* Banner.

SHAGGY IS VEGETARIAN.

NORVILLE ROBERTS is better shown by his well-deserved nickname: Shaggy. He's the always hungry, slovenly dressed, not particularly well-groomed companion of talking dog Scooby-Doo on various Scooby-Doo TV shows and movies. He's always making giant sandwiches and similar snacks, but they never contain meat. That's because the original voice actor for the role, famous DJ Casey Kasem, agreed to the job if he could make the character vegetarian like he was.

SPACE STRETCHES ASTRONAUTS.

IN 2015, NASA sent astronaut Scott Kelly on a year-long mission. To observe the effects of prolonged periods in space on the body, they studied his twin brother, Mark, who remained on Earth. When Scott returned, they compared the two men and found that the guy who'd gone to space had grown two inches in height. The reason: The lack of gravity on the International Space Station stretches the spine, because the space in between vertebrae on the back is usually gently pushed together by gravity.

SANDPAPER IS SANDLESS.

THE TECHNICAL TERM FOR SANDPAPER is "coated abrasives." Some don't use wood-based paper, either, meaning "sandpaper" is quite the misnomer. Those particles that seem like grains of sand are just tiny, tough pieces of rocks or minerals.

PRINCE
IMPROVED
KEYTARS.

IN THE '80s, lots of New Wave and pop bands played "keytars" — electronic keyboards, or synthesizers, that were playable like a guitar. In 1992, the late Prince filed for and received a patent for a new design of a keytar, or a "portable, electronic keyboard musical instrument."

DYLAN
SKIPPED
WOODSTOCK.

AS THE PRE-EMINENT SINGER-SONGWRITER of his generation, Bob Dylan was notably absent from the bill at the Woodstock festival in 1969. Organizers asked him to come, and he said he couldn't because his daughter was sick. However, he lived near the site of the concert, and was thinking about going... until he saw thousands upon thousands of hippies descend on his community. He freaked out, and skipped town to get some peace.

SATURN

RAINS

DIAMONDS.

HERE'S A PREPONDERANCE of methane in the
atmosphere of Saturn. It forms into droplets and starts to fall to
the surface of the planet in liquid form. Saturn's hot lightning hits
the raining methane and turns it into what's basically soot, which
hardens as it falls. The tremendous pressure of that turns it into
blackened graphite as it hits the surface, and then, before long, into
diamonds. About a thousand tons worth of diamonds wash up on
Saturn each year.